Perverted Proverbs: A Manual Of Immorals For The Many...

Harry Graham

Nabu Public Domain Reprints:

You are holding a reproduction of an original work published before 1923 that is in the public domain in the United States of America, and possibly other countries. You may freely copy and distribute this work as no entity (individual or corporate) has a copyright on the body of the work. This book may contain prior copyright references, and library stamps (as most of these works were scanned from library copies). These have been scanned and retained as part of the historical artifact.

This book may have occasional imperfections such as missing or blurred pages, poor pictures, errant marks, etc. that were either part of the original artifact, or were introduced by the scanning process. We believe this work is culturally important, and despite the imperfections, have elected to bring it back into print as part of our continuing commitment to the preservation of printed works worldwide. We appreciate your understanding of the imperfections in the preservation process, and hope you enjoy this valuable book.

PERVERTED PROVERBS

Perverted Proverbs

Dedicated to

Helen Whitney

Do you recall those bygone days,
When you received with kindly praise
   My bantling book of Rhyme?
Praise undeserved, alas! and yet
How sweet! For, tho' we had not met,
   (Ah! what a waste of time!)
I could the more enjoy such mercies
Since I delighted in *your* verses.

And when a Poet stoops to smile
On some one of the rank and file,
   (Inglorious—if not mute,)
Some groundling bard who craves to
   climb,

PERVERTED PROVERBS

Like me, the dizzy rungs of Rhyme,
   To reach the Golden Fruit;
For one in such a situation
The faintest praise is no damnation.

Parnassus heights must surely pall;
For simpler diet do you call,
   Of nectar growing tired?
These verses to your feet I bring,
Drawn from an unassuming spring,
   Well-meant—if not inspired;
O charming Poet's charming daughter,
Descend and taste my toast and water!

For you alone these lines I write,
That, reading them, your brow may light
   Beneath its crown of bays;
Your eyes may sparkle like a star,
With friendship, that is dearer far
   Than any breath of praise;

PERVERTED PROVERBS

The which a lucky man possessing
Can ask no higher human blessing.

And, though the "salt estranging sea"
Be widely spread 'twixt you and me,
   We have what makes amends;
And since I am so glad of you,
Be glad of me a little, too,
   Because of being friends.
And, if I earn your approbation,
Accept my humble dedication.

H. G.

PERVERTED PROVERBS

Foreword

THE Press may pass my Verses by
   With sentiments of indignation,
And say, like Greeks of old, that I
   Corrupt the Youthful Generation;
I am unmoved by taunts like these—
(And so, I think, was Socrates).

Howe'er the Critics may revile,
   I pick no journalistic quarrels,
Quite realizing that my Style
   Makes up for any lack of Morals;
For which I feel no shred of shame—
(And Byron would have felt the same).

I don't intend a Child to read
   These lines, which are not for the Young;
For, if I did, I should indeed
   Feel fully worthy to be hung.

PERVERTED PROVERBS

(Is "hanged" the perfect tense of
   "hang"?
Correct me, Mr. Andrew Lang!)

O Young of Heart, tho' in your prime,
   By you these Verses may be seen!
Accept the Moral with the Rhyme,
   And try to gather what I mean.
But, if you can't, it won't hurt me!
(And Browning would, I know, agree.)

Be reassured, I have not got
   The style of Stephen Phillips' heroes,
Nor Henry Jones's pow'r of Plot,
   Nor wit like Arthur Wing Pinero's!
(If so, I should not waste my time
In writing you this sort of rhyme.)

I strive to paint things as they Are,
   Of Realism the true Apostle;
All flow'ry metaphors I bar,

PERVERTED PROVERBS

Nor call the homely thrush a "throstle."
Such synonyms would make me smile.
(And so they would have made Carlyle.)

My Style may be at times, I own,
   A trifle cryptic or abstruse;
In this I do not stand alone,
   And need but mention, in excuse,
A thousand world-familiar names,
From Meredith to Henry James.

From these my fruitless fancy roams
   To seek the Ade of Modern Fable,
From Doyle's or Hemans' "Stately Ho(l)mes,"
   To t'other of The Breakfast Table;
Like Galahad, I wish (in vain)
"My wit were as the wit of Twain!"

Had I but Whitman's rugged skill,
   (And managed to escape the Censor),

PERVERTED PROVERBS

The Accuracy of a Mill,
   The Reason of a Herbert Spencer,
The literary talents even
Of Sidney Lee or Leslie Stephen.

The pow'r of Patmore's placid pen,
   Or Watson's gift of execration,
The sugar of Le Gallienne,
   Or Algernon's Alliteration.
One post there is I'd not be lost in,
—Tho' I might find it most ex-austin'!

Some day, if I but study hard,
   The public, vanquished by my pen'll
Acclaim me as a Minor Bard,
   Like Norman Gale or Mrs. Meynell,
And listen to my lyre a-rippling
Imperial banjo-spasms like Kipling.

Were I a syndicate like K.
   Or flippant scholar like Augustine;

PERVERTED PROVERBS

Had I the style of Pater, say,
   Which ev'ryone would put their trust in,
I'd love (as busy as a squirrel)
To pate, to kipple, and to birrel.

So don't ignore me. If you should,
   'Twill touch me to the very heart oh!
To be as much misunderstood
   As once was Andrea del Sarto;
Unrecognized to toil away,
Like Millet—not, of course, Mill*ais*.

And, pray, for Morals do not look
   In this unique agglomeration,
—This unpretentious little book
   Of Infelicitous Quotation.
I deem you foolish if you do,
(And Mr. Russell thinks so, too).

PERVERTED PROVERBS

"Virtue is Its Own Reward"

VIRTUE its own reward?   Alas!
   And what a poor one as a rule!
Be Virtuous and Life will pass
   Like one long term of Sunday-School.
(No prospect, truly, could one find
More unalluring to the mind.)

You may imagine that it pays
   To practise Goodness.   Not a bit!
You cease receiving any praise
   When people have got used to it;
'Tis generally understood
You find it *easy* to be good.

The Model Child has got to keep
   His fingers and his garments white;
In church he may not go to sleep,
   Nor ask to stop up late at night.
In fact he must not ever do
A single thing he wishes to.

PERVERTED PROVERBS

He may not paddle in his boots,
    Like naughty children, at the Sea;
The sweetness of Forbidden Fruits
    Is not, alas! for such as he.
He watches, with pathetic eyes,
His weaker brethren make mud-pies.

He must not answer back, oh no!
    However rude grown-ups may be,
But keep politely silent, tho'
    He brim with scathing repartee;
For nothing is considered worse
Than scoring off Mamma or Nurse.

He must not eat too much at meals,
    Nor scatter crumbs upon the floor;
However vacuous he feels,
    He may not pass his plate for more;
—Not tho' his ev'ry organ ache
For further slabs of Christmas cake.

PERVERTED PROVERBS

He is enjoined to choose his food
   From what is easy to digest;
A choice which in itself is good,
   But never what *he* likes the best.
(At times how madly he must wish
For just *one* real unwholesome dish!)

And, when the wretched urchin plays
   With other little girls and boys,
He has to show unselfish ways
   By giving them his choicest toys;
His ears he lets them freely box,
Or pull his lubricated locks.

His face is always being washed,
   His hair perpetually brushed,
And thus his brighter side is squashed,
   His human instincts warped and crushed;
Small wonder that his early years
Are filled with "thoughts too deep for tears."

PERVERTED PROVERBS

He is commanded not to waste
   The fleeting hours of childhood's
     days
By giving way to any taste
   For circuses or matinées;
For him the entertainments planned
Are "Lectures on the Holy Land."

He never reads a story book
   By Rider H. or Winston C.,
In vain upon his desk you'd look
   For tales by Richard Harding D.;
Nor could you find upon his shelf
The works of Rudyard—or myself!

He always fears that he may do
   Some action that is *infra dig.*,
And so he lives his short life through
   In the most noxious rôle of Prig.
("Short life" I say, for it's agreed
The Good die very young indeed.)

PERVERTED PROVERBS

Ah me! How sad it is to think
   He could have lived like me—or you!
With practice and a taste for drink,
   Our joys he might have known, he too!
And shared the pleasure *we* have had
In being gloriously bad!

The Naughty Boy gets much delight
   From doing what he should not do;
But, as such conduct isn't Right,
   He sometimes suffers for it, too.
Yet, what's a spanking to the fun
Of leaving vital things Undone?

If he's notoriously bad,
   But for a day should change his ways,
His parents will be all so glad,
   They'll shower him with gifts and praise!

[15]

PERVERTED PROVERBS

PERVERTED PROVERBS

(It pays a connoisseur in crimes
To be a perfect saint at times.)

Of course there always lies the chance
   That he is charged with being ill,
And all his innocent romance
   Is ruined by a rhubarb pill.
(Alas! 'Tis not alone the Good
That are so much misunderstood.)

But, as a rule, when he behaves
   (Evincing no malarial signs),
His friends are all his faithful slaves,
   Until he once again declines
With easy conscience, more or less,
To undiluted wickedness.

The Wicked flourish like the bay,
   At Cards or Love they always win,
Good Fortune dogs their steps all day,
   They fatten while the Good grow thin.

PERVERTED PROVERBS

The Righteous Man has much to bear;
The Bad becomes a Bullionaire!

For, though he be the greatest sham,
   Luck favours him his whole life through;
At "Bridge" he always makes a Slam
   After declaring "Sans atout";
With ev'ry deal his fate has planned
A hundred Aces in his hand.

And it is always just the same;
   He somehow manages to win,
By mere good fortune, any game
   That he may be competing in.
At Golf no bunker breaks his club,
For him the green provides no "rub."

At Billiards, too, he flukes away
   (With quite unnecessary "side");

PERVERTED PROVERBS

No matter what he tries to play,
   For him the pockets open wide;
He never finds both balls in baulk,
Or makes miss-cues for want of chalk.

He swears; he very likely bets;
   He even wears a flaming necktie;
Inhales Egyptian cigarettes
   And has a "Mens Inconscia Recti";
Yet, spite of all, one must confess
That naught succeeds like his excess.

There's no occasion to be Just,
   No need for motives that are fine,
To be Director of a Trust,
   Or Manager of a Combine;
Your corner is a public curse,
Perhaps; but it will fill your purse.

Then stride across the Public's bones,
   Crush all opponents under you,

PERVERTED PROVERBS

Until you " rise on stepping-stones
   Of their dead selves"; and, when
      you do,
The widow's and the orphan's tears
Shall comfort your declining years!

But having had your boom in oil,
   And made your millions out of it,
Would you propose to cease from toil?
   Great Vanderfeller! Not a bit!
You've *got* to labour, day and night,
Until you die—and serve you right!

Then, when you stop this frenzied race,
   And others in your office sit,
You'll leave the world a better place,
   —The better for your leaving it!
For there's a chance perhaps your heir
May spend what you've collected there.

Myself, how lucky I must be,
   That need not fear so gross an end;

PERVERTED PROVERBS

Since Fortune has not favoured me
   With many million pounds to spend.
(Still, did that fickle Dame relent,
I'd show you how they *should* be
   spent!)

I am not saint enough to feel
   My shoulder ripen to a wing,
Nor have I wits enough to steal
   His title from the Copper King;
And there's a vasty gulf between
The Man I Am and Might Have Been;

But tho' at dinner I may take
   Too much of Heidsick (extra dry),
And underneath the table make
   My simple couch just where I lie,
My mode of roosting on the floor
Is just a trick and nothing more.

And when, not Wisely but too Well,
   My thirst I have contrived to quench,

PERVERTED PROVERBS

The stories I am apt to tell
   May be, perhaps, a trifle French;
(For 'tis in anecdote, no doubt,
That what's Bred in the Beaune comes
     out.)

It does not render me unfit
   To give advice, both wise and right,
Because I do not follow it
   Myself as closely as I might;
There's nothing that I wouldn't do
To point the proper road to *you*.

And this I'm sure of, more or less,
   And trust that you will all agree,
The Elements of Happiness
   Consist in being—just like Me;
No sinner, nor a saint perhaps,
But—well, the very best of chaps.

Share the Experience I have had,
   Consider all I've known and seen,

PERVERTED PROVERBS

And Don't be Good, and Don't be Bad,
  But cultivate a Golden Mean.

   .   .   .   .   .   .

What makes Existence *really* nice
Is Virtue—with a dash of Vice.

" Enough is as Good as a Feast."

WHAT is Enough? An idle dream!
   One cannot have enough, I swear,
Of Ices or Meringues-and-Cream,
   Nougat or Chocolate Eclairs,
Of Oysters or of Caviar,
Of Prawns or Paté de Foie *Grar!*

Who would not willingly forsake
   Kindred and Home, without a fuss,
For Icing from a Birthday Cake,
   Or juicy fat Asparagus,
And journey over countless seas
For New Potatoes and Green Peas?

They say that a Contented Mind
   Is a Continual Feast;—but where
The mental frame, and how to find,
   Which can with Turtle Soup compare?

PERVERTED PROVERBS

No mind, however full of Ease,
Could be Continual Toasted Cheese.

For dinner have a sole to eat,
   (Some Perrier Jouet, '92,)
An Entrée then (and, with the meat,
   A bottle of Lafitte will do),
A quail, a glass of port (just one),
Liqueurs and coffee, and you've done.

But should you want a hearty meal,
   And not this gourmet's lightsome snack,
Fill up with terrapin and teal,
   Clam chowder, crabs and canvas-back;
With all varieties of sauce,
And diff'rent wines for ev'ry course.

Your tastes may be of simpler type;—
   A homely glass of " half-and-half,"

PERVERTED PROVERBS

An onion and a dish of tripe,
    Or headpiece of the kindly calf.
(Cruel perhaps, but then, you know,
"*'Faut tout souffrir pour être veau!*")

'Tis a mistake to eat too much
    Of any dishes but the best;
And you, of course, should never touch
    A thing you *know* you can't digest;
For instance, lobster;—if you *do*,
Well,—I'm amayonnaised at you!

Let this be your heraldic crest,
    A bottle (chargé) of Champagne,
A chicken (gorged) with salad (dress'd),
    Below, this motto to explain—
"Enough is Very Good, may be;
Too Much is Good Enough for Me!"

PERVERTED PROVERBS

"Don't Buy a Pig in a Poke."

UNSCRUPULOUS Pigmongers will
    Attempt to wheedle and to coax
The ignorant young housewife till
    She purchases her pigs in pokes;
Beasts that have got a Lurid Past,
Or else are far Too Good to Last.

So, should you not desire to be
    The victim of a cruel hoax,
Then promise me, ah! promise me,
    You will not purchase pigs in pokes!
('Twould be an error just as big
To poke your purchase in a pig.)

Too well I know the bitter cost,
    To turn this subject off with jokes;
How many a fortune has been lost
    By men who purchased pigs in pokes.

PERVERTED PROVERBS

(Ah! think on such when you would talk
With mouths that are replete with pork!)

And, after dinner, round the fire,
   Astride of Grandpa's rugged knee,
Implore your bored but patient sire
   To tell you what a Poke may be.
The fact he might disclose to you—
Which is far more than *I* can do.

. . . . . .

The Moral of The Pigs and Pokes
   Is not to make your choice too quick.
In purchasing a Book of Jokes,
   Pray poke around and take your pick.
Who knows how rich a mental meal
The covers of *this* book conceal?

PERVERTED PROVERBS

"Learn to Take Things Easily."

To these few words, it seems to me,
   A wealth of sound instruction clings;
O Learn to Take things easily—
   Espeshly Other People's Things;
And Time will make your fingers deft
At what is known as Petty Theft.

Your precious moments do not waste;
   Take Ev'rything that isn't tied!
Who knows but you may have a Taste,
   A Gift perhaps, for Homicide,—
(A Mania which, encouraged, thrives
On Taking Other People's Lives).

"Fools and Their Money soon must part!"
   And you can help this on, may be,
If, in the kindness of your Heart,
   You Learn to Take things easily;
And be, with little education,
A Prince of Misappropriation.

PERVERTED PROVERBS

"A Rolling Stone Gathers No Moss."

I NEVER understood, I own,
   What anybody (with a soul)
Could mean by offering a Stone
   This needless warning not to Roll;
And what inducement there can be
To gather Moss I fail to see.

I'd sooner gather anything,
   Like primroses, or news perhaps,
Or even wool (when suffering
   A momentary mental lapse);
But could forego my share of moss,
Nor ever realize the loss.

'Tis a botanical disease,
   And worthy of remark as such;
Lending a dignity to trees,
   To ruins a romantic touch.
A timely adjunct, I've no doubt,
But not worth writing home about.

PERVERTED PROVERBS

Of all the Stones I ever met,
   In calm repose upon the ground,
I really never found one yet
   With a desire to roll around;
Theirs is a stationary rôle,—
(A joke,—and feeble on the whole).

But, if I were a stone, I swear
   I'd sooner move and view the World
Than sit and grow the greenest hair
   That ever Nature combed and curled.
I see no single saving grace
In being known as "Mossyface!"

Instead, I might prove useful for
   A weapon in the hand of Crime,
A paperweight, a milestone, or
   A missile at Election time;
In each capacity I could
Do quite incalculable good.

PERVERTED PROVERBS

When well directed from the Pit,
    I might promote a welcome death,
If fortunate enough to hit
    Some budding Hamlet or Macbeth,
Who twice each day the playhouse fills,—
(For further Notice See Small Bills).

At concerts, too, if you prefer,
    I could prevent your growing deaf,
By silencing the amateur
    Before she reached that upper F.;
Or else, in lieu of half-a-brick,
Restrain some local Kubelik.

Then, human stones, take my advice,
    (As you should always do, indeed);
This proverb may be very nice,
    But don't you pay it any heed,
And, tho' you make the critics cross,
Roll on, and never mind the moss.

PERVERTED PROVERBS

"After Dinner Sit a While; After Supper Walk a Mile."

AFTER luncheon sit awhile,
   'Tis an admirable plan;
After dinner walk a mile—
   But make certain that you *can*.
(Were you not this maxim taught;—
"Good is Wrought by want of Port.")

After dinner think on this;
   Join the ladies with a smile,
And remember that a Miss
   Is as good as any mile.
(Thus you may be led to feel
What Amis felt for Amile.)

Never fear of being shy
   At the houses where you dine;
You'll recover by-and-bye,
   With the second glass of wine;
And can recognize with bliss
That a Meal is not amiss.

PERVERTED PROVERBS

"It is Never Too Late to Mend."

SINCE it can never be too late
   To change your life, or else renew it,
Let the unpleasant process wait
   Until you are *compelled* to do it.
The State provides (and gratis too)
Establishments for such as you.

Remember this, and pluck up heart,
   That, be you publican or parson,
Your ev'ry art must have a start,
   From petty larceny to arson;
And even in the burglar's trade,
The cracksman is not born, but made.

So, if in your career of crime,
   You fail to carry out some "coup",
Then try again a second time,
   And yet again, until you *do*;
And don't despair, or fear the worst,
Because you get found out at first.

PERVERTED PROVERBS

Perhaps the battle will not go,
   On all occasions, to the strongest;
You may be fairly certain tho'
   That He Laughs Last who laughs the Longest.
So keep a good reserve of laughter,
Which may be found of use hereafter.

Believe me that, howe'er well meant,
   A Good Resolve is always brief;
Don't let your precious hours be spent
   In turning over a new leaf.
Such leaves, like Nature's, soon decay,
And then are only in the way.

The Road to—well, a certain spot,
   (A Road of very fair dimensions),
Has, so the proverb tells us, got
   A parquet-floor of Good Intentions.
Take care, in your desire to please,
You do not add a brick to these.

PERVERTED PROVERBS

For there may come a moment when
   You shall be mended willy-nilly,
With many more misguided men,
   Whose skill is undermined with skilly.
Till then procrastinate, my friend;
" It *Never* is Too Late to Mend!"

"*A Bad Workman Complains of his Tools.*"

THIS Pen of mine is simply grand,
   I never loved a pen so much;
This Paper (underneath my hand)
   Is really a delight to touch;
And never in my life, I think,
Did I make use of finer ink.

The Subject upon which I write
   Is everything that I could choose;
I seldom knew my Wits more bright,
   More cosmopolitan my Views;
Nor ever did my Head contain
So surplus a supply of Brain!

"A Bad Workman Complains of his Tools."

THIS Pen of mine is simply grand,
I never loved a pen so much;
This Paper (underneath my hand)
Is really a delight to touch.
And never in my life, I think,
Did I make use of finer ink.

The subject upon which I write
Is everything that I could choose;
I seldom knew my Wits more bright,
More cosmopolitan my Views;
Nor ever did my Head contain
So surplus a supply of Brain.

PERVERTED PROVERBS

Potpourri.

THERE are many more Maxims to which
   I would like to accord a front place,
But alas! I have got
To omit a whole lot,
   For the lack of available space;
And the rest I am forced to boil down
   and condense
To the following Essence of Sound
   without Sense:

Now the Pitcher that journeys too oft
   To the Well will get broken at last.
But you'll find it a fact
That, by using some tact,
   Such a danger as this can be past.
(There's an obvious way, and a simple,
   you'll own,
Which is, if you're a Pitcher, to Let
   Well alone.)

PERVERTED PROVERBS

Half a loafer is never well-bred,
   And Self-Praise is a Dangerous Thing.
And the Mice are at play
When the Cat is away,
   For a moment, inspecting a King.
(Tho' if Care kills a Cat, as the Proverbs declare,
It is right to suppose that the King will take care.)

Don't Halloo till you're out of the Wood,
   When a Stitch in Good Time will save nine,
While a Bird in the Hand
Is worth Two, understand,
   In the Bush that Needs no Good Wine.
(Tho' the two, if they *Can* sing but Won't, have been known,
By an accurate aim to be killed with one Stone.)

PERVERTED PROVERBS

Never Harness the Cart to the Horse;
   Since the latter should be *à la carte*.
And Birds of a Feather
Come Flocking Together,
   Because they can't well Flock Apart.
(You may cast any Bread on the Waters,
    I think,
But, unless I'm mistaken, you can't make it Sink.)

It is only the Fool who remarks
   That there Can't be a Fire without Smoke;
Has he never yet learned
How the gas can be turned
   On the best incombustible coke?
(Would you value a man by the checks on his suits,
And forget "*que c'est le premier passbook qui Coutts?*")

PERVERTED PROVERBS

Now "*De Mortuis Nil Nisi Bonum*," is Latin, as ev'ryone owns;
If your domicile be
Near a Mortuaree,
    You should always avoid throwing bones.
(I would further remark, if I could,
    —but I couldn't—
That People Residing in Glasshouses shouldn't.)

You have heard of the Punctual Bird,
    Who was First in presenting his Bill;
But I pray you'll be firm,
And remember the Worm
    Had to get up much earlier still;
(So that, if you *can't* rise in the morning, then Don't;
And be certain that Where there's a Will there's a Won't.)

PERVERTED PROVERBS

You can give a bad name to a Dog,
   And hang him by way of excuse;
Whereas Hunger, of course,
Is by far the Best Sauce
   For the Gander as well as the Goose.
(But you shouldn't judge anyone just
   by his looks,
For a Surfeit of Broth ruins too many
   Cooks.)

With the fact that Necessity knows
   Nine Points of the Law, you'll agree.
There are just as Good Fish
To be found on a Dish
   As you ever could catch in the Sea.
(You should Look ere you Leap on a
   Weasel Asleep,
And I've also remarked That Still
   Daughters Run Cheap.)

PERVERTED PROVERBS

The much trodden-on Lane *will* Turn,
   And a Friend is in Need of a Friend;
But the Wisest of Saws,
Like the Camel's Last Straws,
   Or the Longest of Worms, have an end.
So, before out of Patience a Virtue you make,
A decisive farewell of these maxims we'll take.

PERVERTED PROVERBS

Envoi.

"Don't Look a Gifthorse in the Mouth"

I KNEW a man, who lived down South;
   He thought this maxim to defy;
He looked a Gifthorse in the Mouth;
   The Gifthorse bit him in the Eye!
And, while the steed enjoyed his bite,
My Southern friend mislaid his sight.

Now, had this foolish man, that day,
   Observed the Gifthorse in the *Heel*,
It might have kicked his brains away,
   But that's a loss he would not feel;
Because you see (need I explain?)
My Southern friend had got no brain.

When anyone to you presents
   A poodle, or a pocketknife,

PERVERTED PROVERBS

I.

"Don't Look a Giftthorse in the Mouth".

I KNEW a man, who lived down South,
He thought this maxim to defy,
He looked a Giftthorse in the Mouth;
The Giftthorse bit him in the Eye!
And, while the steed enjoyed his bite,
My Southern friend mislaid his sight.

Now, had this foolish man, that day,
Observed the Giftthorse in the Heel,
It might have kicked his brains away,
But that's a loss he would not feel;
Because you see (need I explain?)
My Southern friend had got no brain.

When anyone to you presents
A pencil, or a pocketknife,

PERVERTED PROVERBS

A set of Ping-pong instruments,
   A banjo or a Lady-wife,
'Tis churlish, as I understand,
To grumble that they're second-hand.

And he who termed Ingratitude
   As "worser nor a servant's tooth"
Was evidently well imbued
   With all the elements of Truth;
(While he who said "Uneasy lies
The tooth that wears a crown" was
     wise).

"One must be poor," George Eliot
     said,
   "To know the luxury of giving;"
So too one really should be dead
   To realize the joy of living.
(I'd sooner be—I don't know which—
I'd *like* to be alive and rich!)

PERVERTED PROVERBS

A set of Ping-pong instruments,
A banjo or a Lady-wife,
'Tis churlish, as I understand,
To grumble that they're second-hand.

And he who termed Ingratitude
As "worser nor a servant's tooth"
Was evidently well imbued
With all the elements of Truth;
(While he who said "Uneasy lies
The head that wears a crown" was
    wise).

"One must be poor," George Eliot
    said,
"To know the luxury of giving;"
So too one really should be dead
To realize the joy of living.
(I'd sooner be—I don't know which—
I'd as lief to be alive and rich).

[44]

PERVERTED PROVERBS

This book may be a Gifthorse too,
    And one you surely ought to prize;
If so, I beg you, read it through
    With kindly and uncaptious eyes,
Not grumbling because this particular
    line doesn't happen to scan,
And this one doesn't rhyme!

PERVERTED PROVERBS

Aftword.

'TIS done! We reach the final page,
   With feelings of relief, I'm certain;
And there arrives at such a stage,
   The moment to ring down the curtain.
(This metaphor is freely taken
From Shakespeare—or perhaps from Bacon.)

The Book perused, our Future brings
   A plethora of blank to-morrows,
When memories of Happier Things
   Will be our Sorrow's Crown of Sorrows.
(I trust you recognize this line
As being Tennyson's, not mine.)

PERVERTED PROVERBS

My verses may indeed be few,
   But are they not, to quote the poet,
"The sweetest things that ever grew
   Beside a human door"? I know it.
(What an *in*human door would be,
Enquire of Wordsworth, please, not me.)

'Twas one of my most cherished dreams
   To write a Moral Book some day;
What says the Bard? "The best laid schemes
   Of Mice and Men gang aft agley!"
(The Bard here mentioned, by the bye,
Is Robbie Burns, of course—not I.)

And tho' my pen records each thought
   As swift as the phonetic Pitman,
Morality is not my "forte,"
   O Camarados! (*vide* Whitman)

PERVERTED PROVERBS

And, like the Porcupine, I still
Am forced to ply a fretful quill.

We may be Master of our Fate,
   (As Henley was inspired to mention)
Yet am I but the Second Mate
   Upon the ss. "Good Intention";
For me the course direct is lacking—
I have to do a deal of tacking.

To seek for Morals here's a task
   Of which you well may be despairing;
"What has become of them?" you ask,
   They've given us the slip—like Waring.
"Look East!" said Browning once, and I
Would make a similar reply.

PERVERTED PROVERBS

Look East, where in a garret drear,
  The Author works, without cessation,
Composing verses for a merely nominal remuneration;
And, while he has the strength to write 'em,
Will do so still—*ad infinitum*.

FINIS.

PERVERTED PROVERBS

Look, Dad, where's a garret dress,
The Author writes, without cessa-
  tion;
"Composing verses for a mere-
  ly nominal remuneration;
And, while he has the strength to
  write on,
Will do so still—ad infinitum.